N.Y.) Metropolitan Museum of Art (New York, Luigi Palma di
Cesnola

**A descriptive atlas of the Cesnola collection of Cypriote antiquities**

**in the Metropolitan Museum of Art**

N.Y.) Metropolitan Museum of Art (New York, Luigi Palma di Cesnola

**A descriptive atlas of the Cesnola collection of Cypriote antiquities in the Metropolitan Museum of Art**

ISBN/EAN: 9783741162800

Manufactured in Europe, USA, Canada, Australia, Japa

Cover: Foto ©Thomas Meinert / pixelio.de

Manufactured and distributed by brebook publishing software (www.brebook.com)

N.Y.) Metropolitan Museum of Art (New York, Luigi Palma di
Cesnola

**A descriptive atlas of the Cesnola collection of Cypriote antiquities**

**in the Metropolitan Museum of Art**

# A DESCRIPTIVE ATLAS

OF THE

## CESNOLA COLLECTION

OF

# CYPRIOTE ANTIQUITIES

IN THE

Metropolitan Museum of Art, New York

## LOUIS P. DI CESNOLA, LL.D.

v. 2

NEW YORK

THE METROPOLITAN MUSEUM OF ART

1894

# PLATE XCI.

Vases found at Alambra, or at Ayia Paraskeve. All of red ware; none of them made on a wheel.

779. Height, 13 inches; greatest diameter, about 14 inches; diameter at mouth, 11½ inches.

Nearly globular vessel, with handle and spout; the latter nearly cylindrical, flaring a little at the lip, and reinforced by a brace joining the body of the vessel at the mouth. About the mouth, outside, a beaded rim notched by incised strokes.

780. Height, exclusive of spout, 11 inches; the spout and handles extending about an inch higher; greatest diameter, about 13½ inches; diameter at mouth, 11 inches.

Nearly globular vessel, with handle and double spout, the latter flaring somewhat at the lips. Decorated with a row of disks about 2½ inches below the mouth; three disks on each side; the middle ones each 1 inch in diameter, the others each ⅝ inch. (In other specimens rosettes take the place of these plain disks.) Handle divided near the top, joining the lip in two places; decorated with a longitudinal depression near the division, and with deep transverse indentations on each of its branches. The two spouts separate, their centres about 3 inches apart; joined in front by a thick bar, and supported above by an arch which joins the body as one piece, but branches to meet each spout.

781. Height, 14¾ inches; diameter at mouth, 11½ inches; greatest diameter about 13 inches.

Large vase; ovoid body, with small flat place on bottom; mouth a little flaring; handle on one side, with double spout opposite; the two spouts curving slightly inward toward the body, and with slightly flaring mouths; their centres 3½ inches apart. On one side, midway between handle and spout, a blind spout (or handle), shaped like a real one, but a little smaller. Portion of the main lip of the vessel, and slight portions of the lips of the spouts, broken away.

*PLATE XCI. CONTINUED.*

782. Height, 21½ inches.

Large vase with oval body, cylindrical neck, and handle; mouth slightly flaring. Handle decorated with oblique, transverse, indented strokes, in three bands, crossing alternately in opposite directions, giving the effect of a handle wound with cords or osiers. Neck decorated with a double zigzag of indented strokes, each stroke about 2¾ inches long, running, in front, from mouth to body, and in the rear from mouth to handle; the angles and ends of the zigzags decorated each with three round indentations. Surface somewhat checked and decayed.

783. Height, 19¾ inches.

Vase with ovate body, and long tapering neck; somewhat flaring mouth; handle on one side, opposite which, at junction of neck and body, is a small, pierced ear. Neck decorated with spiral cord in relief; on the body, below the neck, and on either side, a little distance from the handle, a serpentine cord in relief, about 3½ inches long.

784. Height, 4¾ inches; diameter at top, 14 inches, exclusive of spout.

Pan, or wide bowl; outline that of a rudely globular segment; irregular flat place, of about 3 inches diameter, on the bottom. On one side a trough, or open spout, projects about 2 inches; opposite this, a vertical projection, with a notch at top in the direction of the spout; and also, about an inch below the edge, a horizontal process about 4 inches long, in which are two holes, apparently for suspension. One or two small chipped places.

785. Height, 7 inches; diameter at top, 18 inches.

Circular bowl or pan of the general shape of a spherical segment; with a small flat place on the bottom. On the edge, opposite each other, two projections, each with two holes, as if for suspension or the insertion of cords for handles. At the middle of each, and also at six other points on the edge, small spurs; the eight equi-distant from each other. A few small nicks on the edge.

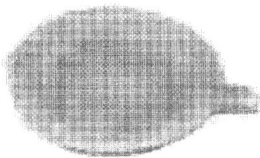

# PLATE XCII.

Red ware, found at Alambra or Ayia Paraskeve; none made on a wheel.

786. Height, 3¾ inches.

Cup of hemispherical shape, with 6 equidistant ears on the lip, projecting outward and slightly upward. A little incrusted and discolored.

787. Extreme length, 9½ inches; diameter, 5½ inches.

Cup, a spherical segment with loop-shaped handle, the latter strengthened by a cross-bar. Handle broken across and reset.

788. Height, 2¼ inches, exclusive of handle.

Vase, much like a modern teapot. Body, nearly a spherical segment; decoration an incised zigzag about the top, with punctured dots near the angles. Handle reaching about ⅓ higher than the rest of the vase; spout, opposite the handle, a round pipe curved upward nearly to the level of the body. Surface somewhat incrusted.

789. Height, 3½ inches.

Small pitcher-like vase (œnochoë), with handle and no spout. Body globular, neck cylindrical. Outside a little incrusted.

790. Height, 7 inches.

Ovoid, almost globular vase, with recurved or slightly flaring lip; very heavy handle; opposite the latter a projection about ¼ inch below the lip, as if for steadying with the fingers.

791. Height, 3½ inches.

Vase with somewhat obovate or pear-shaped body, tapering neck, and slightly flaring mouth; handle a mere pierced ear at junction of neck and body. The ear had a vertical projection at the outer corner; but in this specimen the angle has been worn off.

792. Height, 6¾ inches.

Vase with nearly globular body; round, curved spout at the side; a little above this spout,

*PLATE XCII. CONTINUED.*

6 equidistant pierced ears, as if for a cord. At top, long neck, joined by a handle which extends to the body ; above the handle, spout curved slightly towards the other spout, and open on upper side. Just above where handle joins body an incurved portion breaks the outline of the body ; and at junction of neck and body, opposite the handle, is another pierced ear. Surface much worn. Both spouts broken at ends, the upper one along its edges also. One of the pierced ears broken.

    793. Height, 2¾ inches ; or with handle, 4 inches.

    Cup (cyathus), nearly hemispherical ; handle formed of an arched strip of clay, joined to body just below the lip, decorated at top by 4 vertical incised marks. Opposite handle, 2 slight projections outside of the unbroken edge of the lip, where a spout might have been expected.

    794. Height, 5 inches.

    Vase of rudely globular body ; long, nearly cylindrical neck, flaring at mouth ; handle extending from mouth to body. Decorated with incised lines, as shown in the plate.

# PLATE XCIII,

All of red ware, glazed, not made on a wheel ; found at Alambra, or Ayia Paraskeve.

795.   Height, 6 inches.

Vase, with nearly globular body ; nearly cylindrical neck, and slightly flaring mouth ; handle, joining neck midway of its length ; opposite the handle, tapering pipe-spout, curving slightly upwards.   Surface somewhat decayed.

796.   Height, 11½ inches.

Vase with compressed ovoid body, the edge turned towards the spectator in the plate ; nearly cylindrical neck, curved outward at top and bottom ; flaring lip, recurved and compressed at one point, with an open nozzle.   Handle with upward projection at top.   On the neck, opposite the handle, and at two places on the body below, in the same vertical line, little pierced projections, or ears ; likewise two such pierced ears in the line below the handle, and three on each edge of the compressed body.   Decoration of incised lines, in circles and oblique bands on the neck, and vertical bands and zigzags on the body.

797.   Height, 5¾ inches.

Vase with pear-shaped body ; narrow, cylindrical neck, and wide flaring lips ; handle. Decorated with incised lines in geometrical patterns, as shown in the plate.   Handle broken off, and reset.

798.   Height, 2 inches ; or with handle, 4 inches ; diameter at top, 6⅛ inches.

Cup (cyathus) in shape of a spherical segment ; handle joined at edge, with slight projection at its top corners, and decorated with 4 incised lines at top.   About lip, 6 slight projections, which, with the ends of the handles, divide the circumference into 8 equal parts.

799.   Height, 3 inches ; diameter at top, 8 inches.

Dish in shape of spherical segment ; on one side a large, round, curved spout with somewhat flaring mouth, and joined to the side of the vessel a little above its middle height.   Opposite

*PLATE XCIII. CONTINUED.*

this, just below the edge, a horizontal projection with a hole for suspension; on each side, midway between this projection and the spout, 3 projections on the edge. Somewhat discolored.

800.  Height, 3 inches; diameter at top, 8 inches.

Dish in shape of spherical segment; open spout or nozzle on one side at top; opposite which is a heavy handle, set on the edge, with a vertical incised mark on its inside at top.

801.  Height, 5 inches.

Cup with foot; body shaped like half an egg; foot cylindrical, tapering above and below. Through the foot, about ⅔ the distance from base to body, a small hole pierced, as if for suspension.

802.  Height, 2¼ inches; diameter at top, 4¾ inches.

Nearly hemispherical cup; semi-cylindrical open spout at top, about 1 inch long; opposite this a small pierced ear, for a handle. Decorated with incised lines in geometrical patterns; about the top, 2 double lines, the space between which is occupied by sets of triple cross-lines, making a truss-work almost like a zigzag; from this band an ornamentation of like structure descends vertically to the bottom, doubled at spout and handle, but single midway between them; the 4 spaces between being occupied by patterns of concentric circles.

803.  Height, 3 inches; or with handle, 4½ inches; diameter, 4¼ inches.

Cup of nearly hemispherical shape; handle attached with its ends on a horizontal line; opposite it a round spout, slightly curving upwards; below the edge, 3 raised buttons on each side. Lip and end of spout somewhat chipped.

# PLATE XCIV.

All red ware; glazed originally; decorated (if at all) with incised lines in geometrical pattern; not made on a wheel; found near Alambra or at Ayia Paraskeve.

804.  Height, 8 inches.

Amphora-shaped vase, with slightly ovate body, and very wide cylindrical neck, flaring slightly at top. Handles with projecting ears above. The edge slightly nicked and broken.

805.  Height, 8½ inches; greatest diameter, 4¾ inches.

Vessel with nearly globular body; nearly cylindrical neck, joined midway of its length by a handle; opposite the handle a pipe-spout, tapering and curved upwards. Above the handle a little slit in the side of the neck, extending from the mouth ⅝ inch downwards, ⅛ inch wide at top, and $\frac{1}{16}$ inch wide at bottom. A few slight chips here and there, and some incrustation.

806.  Height, 9½ inches.

Vase of rather obovate body, cylindrical neck with slightly flaring base and mouth, handle joining neck at its middle. Decorated with raised bands, straight and zigzag, about neck and body, and along handle.

807.  Height, 4¼ inches; diameter at top, 11½ inches.

Large dish or pan, in shape of spherical segment, a little flattened at the bottom on the outside; large wide trough-nozzle at one side, with lip curved downward at the extremity; opposite this a projection with a hole for suspension. Some vases of this sort have a thicker projection, pierced with two holes, through both projection and body.

808.  Height, 7¼ inches; globular diameter, about 5 inches.

Nearly globular vase, with cylindrical neck slightly flaring at the mouth; and a handle. Outside nearly black in places, apparently from the firing. Cracked, but not broken.

809.  Height, 9¾ inches.

*PLATE XCIV. CONTINUED.*

Amphora-shaped vase ; body nearly globular ; neck long, nearly cylindrical, flaring a little at the top ; handles merely pierced ears at junction of neck and body. Decorated, as shown in the plate.

810.   Height, $8\frac{1}{8}$ inches ; greatest diameter, about $5\frac{1}{2}$ inches.

Vase of nearly the same description as the last, but neck larger in proportion ; the whole ruder ; and the decoration in different patterns.

# PLATE XCV.

—   —

Vases of curious pattern; all found at Dali Potamia except No. 814, which was found at Curium, and No. 818, which was found at Dali. All of red or gray ware, but colored externally white, or grayish white, with decoration generally in brown.

811.   Red ware, extreme height, 5¾ inches; extreme length, 5¼ inches.

Vase in rude form of antlered deer. Body in the form of a full sack, supported by 4 short legs; head short, ears large, antlers thick, branches simple; tail projecting in a line with the curve of the back. Mouth of vase, a spout rising just above and before the tail, ending in a long trough-nozzle. Handle, on the back, a mere projection with hole for suspension. Eyes, mere punctured holes, or dots, with rings of brown about them; ears also with punctured holes. Decoration in brown; chequer-work on breast; vertical and horizontal lines on sides; five bands about the spout; lines vertical, straight, zigzag, and curving, in the rear; stripes along tail and antlers; wide bands about legs, and wide streaks down them, the latter joining a wide horizontal band about the lower part of the body. Wide cross under the belly.

812.   Height, 6¼ inches; length, 10 inches.

Gray ware. Vase in rude shape of fish; mouth of vase in middle of back, the lip joining a handle, which extends 2 inches behind the mouth to join the back. Small hole for a spout in fish's mouth. Fish with sharp back, round belly, nearly 4 inches through the widest part, and about 4¾ inches deep at the middle. Stands on 4 stumpy legs. Two ill-shaped fins on each side. Eyes, round lumps of clay, colored red. Red mark to indicate opening of gill-covers. Tail broken away; slight chippings off mouth of vase.

813.   Gray ware. Height, about 11 inches.

Vase in general form of a goblet, but closed with ellipsoidal top, above which is a handle, and also a spout in the shape of an antelope's neck and head; the horns curving back to meet the handle near its middle. Vase open at bottom, where it may be filled; but not emptied.

*PLATE XCV. CONTINUED.*

When set on its base the water does not run out, but can be poured from the spout as in other vases. This property is secured by an internal cone, extending nearly to the top within. Decoration, bands of brown about the foot and body ; on the top, elliptical band enclosing spout and handle opposite ; the sides of this band joined by 2 straight bands under the handle and at right angles with it ; as also by diagonals to the rude parallelogram thus formed. In the space between this elliptical band and the first circular band about the body, a band of vertical stripes perpendicular to the handle ; between this and the handle ends, nests of triangles having the circular band for a common base ; the inner triangle filled in with crossing lines drawn parallel to the two sides. Eyes and eyelashes of the antelope-spout indicated in brown ; neck decorated with a band about its top and its base, and vertical stripes joining these two bands. Handle colored brown on the sides ; transverse bands on top. Antelope's horns decorated with lines at edges, and short oblique lines across the outside to indicate furrows. Broken in several places, and reset.

814. Red ware, exterior gray. Height, 5¼ inches ; length, 5¼ inches. Found at Curium.

Vase in rude figure of a swan. Body turned on a wheel, and shaped like that of an amphora ; tail flattened laterally ; spout in a projection at breast ; 3 short legs. Neck and head smooth ; short stumpy wings, each chipped a little at the top. Feathers sparingly indicated by incised marks. Handle arching over part of the back, from rear of neck. Behind the rear end of handle, a hole for filling.

815. Gray ware. Height, about 11 inches.

Globular vase with foot ; spout, an antelope's head, much like that of No. 813. Opposite the spout a false one, in all respects similar to the first, but solid. Handle made by the crossing of the horns of the 2 antelopes, which join, on either side, a solid loop attached to the body at the top. Vase has a hole in the bottom, and properties of holding and pouring a liquid, like No. 813. Decoration of foot and lower half of the body, horizontal bands of brown, with one wide band of red in the middle. Wide bands of brown about each antelope's neck ; eyes and noses indicated in brown ; horns with brown lines along edges, and short transverse oblique lines on the sides. Handle-loop brown, enclosed in a rude rectangle whose sides are triple

*PLATE XCV. CONTINUED.*

lines of brown, their ends each a single wide band. From the sides of this rectangle, on either side, descend to the first horizontal band about the globe, two sets of triple lines, between which (on each side) is a diamond of brown lines; its interior dark, but divided into 4 lozenges by a light oblique cross in the middle. From the antelope's neck five lines of brown descend to the first horizontal band. Broken in places, and reset.

816. Gray ware. Extreme height, 5½ inches; extreme diameter, 6¼ inches; inner diameter of ring, 3 inches.

Vase in form of a ring; spout, the rude head and neck of a ram, with spiral horns, set on each side, coiling vertically; the mouth for filling, a funnel set upright, opposite the spout. A handle curves up and across from the funnel to the neck of the spout, its middle elevated as high as the ram's head. Vase stands on 3 short legs. Decoration, about the ring, lozenges, or diamonds, filled in with cross-bars parallel to the sides of the lozenges; the row of lozenges having two bands of brown above and two below them, about the ring; on top of the ring, a row of triangles made of and filled in with slanting lines of brown, their bases resting on the highest band of brown above mentioned. These triangles join and are alternate with a like set, whose bases rest on a band about the inner side of the ring; and the lines that fill in the triangles of the first row are parallel to the right-hand side of the triangles, while those that fill in the triangles of the other row are parallel to the other (left) side of the same triangles of the first row, giving the appearance of plaits, or a wide braid of two compound strands. Neck of ram decorated with patterns of a few perpendicular and horizontal lines, and many oblique lines. Eyes prominent, dark brown; nose with rings or bands of very dark brown; horns with lines and bands of brown; between the horns, a small button, colored with brown. Handle with brown bands, different shades alternating. Funnel with wide bands of brown. Broken, and reset. Small portions broken away from handle, funnel, and tips of horns.

817. Gray ware. Height, 5⅝ inches; length, 6⅜ inches (extreme).

Vase in rude figure of a ram with spreading, curved horns. Body like a full sack; tail short, curved down in a line with back; 4 short legs. Spout, above tail, like that of No. 811. Handle, an arch or ring at middle of back. Body decorated with brown lines, perpendicular and

*PLATE XCV. CONTINUED.*

transverse ; a belt of straight and wavy zigzag lines about the body below the handle. Holes with a circle about them for eyes ; ears far out of place, with holes ; ring about nose ; oblique bands about horns ; perpendicular lines from face to forefoot, the one running through the middle of the leg, wavy ; bands about spout ; wavy lines along handle on each side, a straight one on top. A six-armed cross on back, in front of handle, and another behind it. Wide band on each side of belly, reaching to bottom of each leg ; and wide cross underneath the belly. Left horn a little chipped.

818. Red ware. Length, 6½ inches ; height, extreme, 5 inches. Found at Dali.

Vase in rude form of a bull ; mouth a simple opening behind the fore-shoulders ; handle on back. Small hole for spout in the animal's mouth. Horns and legs slim ; tail hanging straight down, not separate from the body ; eyes, buttons ; dewlap marked. Back and upper parts generally colored brown. Decoration on sides like branching boughs, or else straps with streamers, 3 on each side. Head and shoulders with longitudinal and transverse stripes. Branching stripes on left flank. Right foreleg broken off, and reset ; one eye partly broken away.

819. Red ware. Extreme height, 5¼ inches ; extreme length, 6¼ inches.

Vase in form of crouching lion ; tail curled over back. Spout in centre of back, to which is attached a handle like that of a pitcher ; the other end of handle joining back of neck. Decorated in red and brown stripes, crosswise on limbs, handle, and spout ; lengthwise on the body—where are also wavy lines along the side. A broad band behind the head from one fore-shoulder to the other, which, with the broad band along the sides and about the breast, suggests a harness. Eyes indicated by cones, colored brown. Mouth wide ; holes for nostrils, and another in the middle of the mouth. Paws and forelock indicated by incised marks. Long stripes on the belly, and on each leg. Spout, handle, and one leg, broken off, and reset.

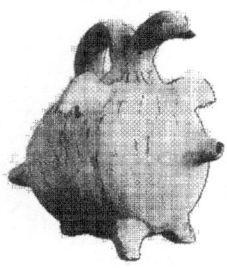

# PLATE XCVI.

— —

All of red ware, decorated (if at all) with incised lines in geometrical patterns; not made on a wheel. Found at Alambra, or Ayia Paraskeve.

820. Height, 8 inches.

Vase in rude imitation of a wine-skin, with handle joining at the mouth. On one side, two button-like prominences, as shown in the plate. The side not shown in the plate is much more convex and capacious.

821. Height, 8¼ inches.

Vase with pear-shaped body, two tapering necks, each flaring into a wide lip at top; a bar joining the two necks nearly midway of their length, from which a handle extends to the body. Opposite the handle, a projection about ¾ inch in height, as wide as the handle. Decorated as stated above, as shown in the plate. One neck broken, and reset; both mouths somewhat chipped.

822. Height, 5 inches.

Nearly globular; spout round, its top cut away about ¾ inch from the body; handle opposite; on the lip, above the spout, a projection; others, about one inch long on each side, in line with top of spout, midway between spout and handle.

823. Length, 5 inches; height, 3¼ inches.

Vessel nearly egg-shaped; oblong hole with rounded corners in the top, over which fitted a cover rectangular with rounded corners, pierced with two holes. On each side of the mouth, two holes, for suspension or for fastening on the cover. Cover and vase both decorated as stated above.

824. Height, 3½ inches; diameter at top, 7 inches.

Nearly hemispherical bowl; with two semi-cylindrical spouts, opposite each other, at the top; midway between them, on each side, two projections with vertical notches inside.

*PLATE XCVI. CONTINUED.*

825.  Extreme height, 9 inches.

Vase of a shape rudely resembling a bird, with handle joining back and neck. The portion of the neck that is above the handle, so cut away as to be an open spout. Tail indicated by a projection; near which, on the back, is still another projection; another is at base of neck, and another on the breast, both pierced. Long raised lines (with cross incised marks), from neck along edge of back to tail, and on the back above them, indicate wings. Three legs. Spout broken, and reset.

826.  Height, 5 inches; length, 7½ inches.

Rudely shaped vase representing an animal; body almost egg-shaped, with pointed projection at tail; neck cylindrical, with flaring mouth. Notched raised line whole length of underside of neck and down to base of body, on which is a pierced projection under the neck; another line from base of neck at top to middle of back, where appear to be the remains of a ring-like handle; from which notched raised lines extend half way down the side. The notched raised lines seem to represent cords.

# PLATE XCVII.

All of very dark colored ware, even black; decorated in geometrical patterns, with incised lines that show a white color; not made on a wheel. Found at Alambra or Ayia Paraskeve.

827. Height, 4 inches.

Vase nearly in shape of a pitcher (œnochoë); body globular, with three legs; neck cylindrical; projection on the lip (no spout), opposite which is a handle. The lip a little chipped.

828. Height, 2 inches; diameter, 3¾ inches.

Small bowl with foot (phiale); shape nearly hemispherical.

829. Height, 4 inches.

Amphora-shaped vase; body nearly globular; cylindrical neck with bead about the lip; pierced ears for handles.

830. Height, 5¼ inches.

Vase with globular body; long tapering neck, at top of which, on one side of the mouth, is a pierced ear.

831. Height, 5½ inches.

Vase in shape of a full round sack, standing on its somewhat flattened base; somewhat tapering towards the top; neck cut away above into an open spout; small pierced ear at base of neck.

832. Height, 3½ inches.

Pitcher-shaped vase (œnochoë); body nearly globular; neck expanding upwards; handle; opposite the latter a small pierced ear.

833. Height, 4¾ inches.

Pitcher-shaped vase (œnochoë); body nearly globular; neck cylindrical, flaring a little at the mouth; handle with spur or projection at top. Remarkable for spiral direction of decoration on the neck.

*PLATE XCVII. CONTINUED.*

834.   Height, 2¾ inches ; diameter, 4 inches.

Nearly hemispherical bowl (phiale) ; projection on the outside where a spout would be looked for, but no spout.

835.   Height, 5 inches.

Vase with globular body, its top drawn up toward a pear shape ; long, tapering neck, and flaring mouth ; handle extending from lip to body.   Mouth slightly chipped.

836.   Height, 2½ inches ; diameter, 4 inches.

Nearly hemispherical bowl (phiale).   Broken in two, and reset.

# Plate XCVIII.

All of red ware; decorated with incised lines in geometrical patterns; not made on a wheel. Found at Alambra or Ayia Paraskeve.

837. Height, 6½ inches.

Vase of same general description as the next, but decoration in different patterns; spout cut abruptly off at the end, instead of curving with rounded corners; handle with a little spur at top; very small ear opposite handle. Handle broken, and reset.

838. Height, 6¼ inches.

Vase (œnochoë) with pear-shaped body; cylindrical neck joined to body at a small angle, its top cut away and inclined so as to form an open curved spout and lip; handle joining neck at top of complete cylinder; opposite the handle, a smaller handle, or ear, at junction of neck and body.

839. Height, about 4 inches; length, 5½ inches.

Vase in rude imitation of an animal; shape of the body like a plummet, or pointed ovoid, the point being at the breast. Tail short, with a little upward inclination; spout cylindrical, flaring at mouth, set obliquely on the body, to which it is joined by a small handle. The four legs fork, each pair from a single shank. Front pair of legs broken, and reset.

840. Height, 5¼ inches.

Vase with globular body; short, cylindrical neck; flaring mouth; handle joining body to mouth, and opposite it a short spur pierced vertically.

841. Height, 3¼ inches.

Vase of nearly globular form; cylindrical mouth; straight, nearly cylindrical pipe for spout; handle joined with ends in the same horizontal line. Much like a modern teapot.

842. Height, 5¾ inches; length, 7 inches.

Vase in rude form of sitting bird, the wings suggested by the decoration, as well as

*PLATE XCVIII. CONTINUED.*

slightly indicated by a raised line extending on each side from neck to tail, and another joining these, passing over the back through the junction of handle and body. The neck of the bird forms the spout, which is cut away above its junction with the handle, to form a trough-spout. Below the neck a spur, whence extends a raised line to a projection at the breast, still further indicating its figure as that of a bird. End of spout broken off on one side.

843. Height, 3½ inches ; length, 6½ inches.

Vase whose form and decoration suggest an oval, pointed purse ; its neck round, curved to one side, where a handle joins neck and body. End of neck and handle broken away ; remnants of handle, and the body also, broken in two, and reset.

# PLATE XCIX.

—

Red ware; strongly glazed; decorations with incised lines in geometrical patterns; not made on a wheel. Found at Alambra or Ayia Paraskeve.

844. Height, 6¼ inches.

Vase (œnochoë?) with globular body; wide cylindrical neck with somewhat flaring lips; handle; opposite the last a pierced ear.

845. Height, 8½ inches.

Vase (œnochoë) with pear-shaped body; nearly cylindrical neck, with slight flare at the mouth; handle with high projecting spur at the top; pierced ear opposite the handle at base of neck.

846. Height, 3¾ inches; diameter at top, 6¾ inches.

Nearly hemispherical bowl (phiale); on the edge, three projections nearly equi-distant one from another; each with a notch across the top in the direction of the edge. Below one of them, on the side, a spur or ear, pierced horizontally.

847. Height, 5 inches; diameter at top, 10½ inches. Bowl whose shape is the segment of an oval; on the edge, equi-distant one from another, four large elevations or ears; their top line a little concave. Below one of these, on the side, a pierced ear.

848. Height, 2¼ inches; diameter at top, 4 inches.

Nearly hemispherical bowl, with pierced ear on one side at top. Chip broken out on the edge.

849. Height, 6½ inches.

Vase with globular body; long tapering neck with slightly flaring mouth; pipe-spout on one side, above which, at base of neck, is a pierced ear; opposite this a handle joining the neck midway of its length. Decoration, two incised wavy lines on each side, extending from a pair of large punctured dots at top of neck to two other like dots on the body, a little lower down than the base of the handle.

*PLATE XCIX. CONTINUED.*

850.   Height, 10 inches.

Vase with pear-shaped body ; long tapering neck with wide flaring mouth ; handle joining neck at middle ; opposite the handle a long projection, not very high.   Neck and handle broken, and reset.

# Plates C., CI.

---

851, 852.   Different views of the same object.   Height, 16⅜ inches; diameter at top, 12⅜ inches; largest diameter, about 13 inches.   Red ware.   Found at Ayia Paraskeve, near Alambra.

Large vase (crater), whose shape, color, and decoration are exhibited in the plates.   Besides that here visible, there is a wide band of red within, reaching half way down the neck; also the flat rim is decorated on top with light strokes in the direction of radii from the centre of the mouth, except at the places where the handles join, and at the points midway between the handles on each side; at each of which four points a diamond, or square panel, divided into four points (like those seen behind the bigæ) replaces the strokes.   The wide red bands about the vase, the double stripe on the outside of the handles, as well as the colored curve about the foot of the handles, need no further description than their display on the plate affords.   The figured zone, about the body of the vase, seems to represent a religious or funeral procession, whose beginning and end are separated by a design seen just ahead of the horses in Plate C., composed of a wavy line (perhaps rudely representing a vine) descending from near the horses' heads to the bottom of the zone, short curves drawn in and concentric with its concave sinuosity on either side.   Next to this, two persons in a *biga*, or chariot with two horses.   The horses with long, heavy, ill-formed bodies, long, arched tails, immense haunches, thin legs, feet so ill-drawn as to seem like rude bird's toes; long necks and high heads; decorated behind the head with three feathers (visible on the head of the nearer horse), and a heavy tuft (almost pompon) on top, inclining backward, in place of ears; heads long and thin, and curved slightly downwards; prominent eyes; the reins from the two heads unite in a common band or ring at the necks, whence four lines or reins extend to the charioteer.

Chariot; body seems to display the two sides with a false perspective, so that the second rider seems to be outside (but the inner visible wall *may* be a partition), though it seems as if the two riders were intended to be abreast in the chariot; wheels with four spokes, no hub represented;

pole extends from top of the chariot between the horses, having a vertical support a little in front of the chariot body, extending to the ground; a step visible behind the wheel. Riders rudely formed; heads crowned; dress decorated with dots arranged in lines (the sides of the chariot body are similarly decorated); the arms of the charioteer being merely forked projections, a horse rein coming to each fork. Above and below the horse-reins are rude *guilloches*, or cord-work, perhaps to indicate clouds or dust. Behind the chariot on a level with the centre of the wheel, a square, or diamond, divided into four parts by crooked cross-lines (or else by two rudely circular arcs tangent to each other, the centres respectively being opposite corners), two of these parts being adorned by short curves concave towards the corners (or concentric short curves).

(This chariot occupies the centre of the space between the handles of the vase on one side, as does the other chariot on the other side of the vase.)

Following the biga is a series of six objects, three on each side of the handle, as follows: two columns, each made of lines bent out nearly at a right angle toward the sides at top, and in the middle a pole or rod extending much higher, bearing at the top what seems to be a standard, or symbol, of tufts and streamers, the whole much like an inverted lyre (without the strings); the first of these columns (with its standard) of the full height of the zone, the next somewhat shorter; then two other, shorter columns, of like structure, but instead of the pole and standard, an Assyro-Phœnician crescent and sun supported on a rod of dots and overarched by a garland of dots or perhaps an arch of stars (these columns not visible on either plate, but like those seen towards the right in Plate C.); then another column with standard, of same height as the second above mentioned; then another column with the crescent, sun, etc., of the full height of the zone. These two not visible on either plate; between them, from the side of the handle, descends a rude curved line, suggesting, and probably intended for, a spiral. The arch of stars over the crescent and sun is a single row of dots on some of the columns; double on the others.

Next follows the biga with horses and two riders shown on Plate CI.; of essentially the same description as the other; but the horse-reins are not so coarse; the *guilloches* less elaborate, and little more than interrupted wavy lines; and behind the chariot is a simple square

or diamond divided into four parts by lines parallel to the sides. Next follow six objects, grouped about the handle similarly to those about the other handle, as follows : a rude, crowned Assyro-Phœnician Astarte (or Aphrodite), of the full height of the zone ; her head crowned, her profile directed towards the chariot ; arms extended and curved towards the head ; body seen in front ; each breast a spiral ; dress a long robe, decorated with transverse stripes. Then five columns (three are seen on the plate) with crescent, sun, and arch of stars, like those above described ; of which, again, some have a double arch and others a single one. The bigæ occupy the central portion of the zone between the handles ; while each handle is in the centre of the six objects beneath and at each side of it, as above stated. Of the six, those beneath the handle are the shortest ; the pair just outside these, a little higher ; and the pair still outside, the full height of the zone. Doubtless the vase is Phœnician, and the decoration entirely oriental, or more strictly Assyro-Phœnician. The columns may suggest *metae*, and trophy or commemorative columns, and the chariots a race ; but our first interpretation seems the more probable.

# PLATES CII., CIII.

853, 854. Gray ware. Height, 14½ inches; diameter at top, 10½ inches; greatest diameter, about 12½ inches. Found at a tomb near Amathus, and Palaeo Limassol.

Vase (crater) of shape much resembling that of Plates C., CI.; but shorter neck and handles, and the expanded portion of the body much greater. Decoration dark brown, as shown in the plates. Within, a band of brown about 2 inches wide; on the flat edge, six sets of parallel lines, in the broad arrow-point shape, all pointing in a direction opposite to that of the motion of the hands of a clock, when looked at from above; each set about 6 inches long. Outside, besides the bands seen in the plates, each handle has three vertical stripes of brown, uniting at the base of the handle.

Design of central zone: four bigæ, each with two riders; two on each side of the vase; all forming one procession, moving in a direction opposite to that on Plates C., CI. Horses, riders, and bigæ of roughly the same description as those on Plates C., CI., but better drawn, and exhibiting more motion; the chariot walls here being clearly seen to be a single curved shell, and one of the riders seeming to be outside by reason of poor perspective. Chariot walls and dress of riders decorated with dots; reins go directly from horses' heads to charioteer's body (he having no arms or hands).

Pole of chariot fastened at top and bottom both of chariot in front, and bending down between the horses. Ears take the place of the tufts seen on the horses' heads in Plates C., CI.; chariot has no step behind. Riders and horses taller and slimmer than in Plates C., CI. Horses have the same three plumes; headstall ornamental, in white; ornamental girths and breast-straps (the latter with tassels), tied at the corners with an immense bow—all in white. Above and below the chariot pole, and beneath the horses, also before the horses of the foremost chariot on Plate CII. (and therefore beneath the handle), are fan-shaped decorations, or rather rude sectors of nests of concentric circles, one of them beneath the chariot pole; the number of them varying from 4 to 6 above the pole, from 4 to 6 (perhaps 8 in one instance, but they are too faded for certainty) beneath the horses.

Stretching from top to bottom of zone, between each two bigæ, except that to the right on Plate CII. and the one before it, are two pairs of wavy lines, roughly parallel, the space between filled in by transverse lines, which are sometimes shaded in bands. Above the horses are spaces decorated in a similar way, i.e., a double wavy line let down in a curve or festoon from the top of the zone, and the space above filled in with close lines. (A precisely similar decoration, alone by itself, occupies the shoulder zone of a vase in the Cesnola collection, of one of the forms shown in Plate XC.)

Above the horses of the biga seen on the right in Plate CIII. is a pair of double wavy lines with the space between filled in as before, and shaded also in bands, making as it were a real festoon of tapestry; while a similar decoration extends from the horse's crupper to the ground, in front of the tails themselves; also with this biga is found the greatest number of fan-ornaments beneath the horses and above the chariot pole; while the chariot walls are distinguished by conspicuous trefoil ornaments at the corners. Ornaments similar to the fan-shaped decoration occur as a colored groundwork on the sarcophagus of Amathus, Vol. I., Plates CXLIX., CL.

# PLATES CIV., CV.

855, 856. Opposite sides of the same object. Gray or light salmon colored ware. Extreme height, 3 feet, 10¾ inches; height to top of vase proper, 2 feet, 9¾ inches; Greatest diameter, about 23 inches. Found in the temple vaults at Curium.

Great vase of nearly ovoid body; neck portion cylindrical; foot curving outwards, with two *tori* about the base. Cover, which rests on a flange within, a flattish conical piece, surmounted by a cylinder, formed at top into an amphora (*kalpis*), with two horizontally set handles on the sides, and one set vertically, joining the neck and body. On the body, just below the neck, four wide, strap-like handles, in the style of an amphora, set equidistant one from another. Decoration: two zones of animal figures about the body, with analogous decoration on the handles and upon the zones of the vase at the top of the cover; the rest in zones and bands of geometrical figures. The latter are more conveniently described first. On the body, below the zones of animal figures: wide and narrow circular horizontal bands, the wide ones singly, the finer in sets of three; disposed among which are five zones occupied by nests of concentric circles, each nest connected with the next by a straight oblique line so as to give the appearance of a succession of spiral volutes; some of the concentric circles being so drawn or blended that the nest seems a large black dot; above and below each of the oblique lines a very small circle, which now and then becomes a dot. About the foot, five horizontal bands; near the top one zone of nests of concentric circles, etc., in all respects similar to those on the body; near the bottom one zone of very fine circles, which are now and then mere dots; at the middle, and occupying about ⅓ of the height of the foot, a zone occupied with pointed elliptical (conventional olive-leaf?) patterns, set vertically, the outline of each double, and the inner face filled in with oblique shading; between each two points, at top and bottom, a very small circle. Cylindrical neck above the handles: rectangles, almost squares, separated by bars of vertical lines, in the midst of which is a close zigzag; the rectangles occupied alternately by chequer-work and by an eight-pointed or foliate star, between each two points of which is a rosette of dots. These rectangles being twenty in number, the handles set at equal distances, fall alternately opposite a rectangle with the star and one with the chequer-work. Cover: conical portion decorated generally like the lower part of the body, but with one wide zone of chequer-work; cylindrical part with five horizontal bands, the middle portion a zone of chequer-work; body of amphora, below and above the handles, five horizontal bands; its lower handles with lines along their length, its upper handles with transverse lines; neck, a zone of rectangles, separated by vertical bars of fine lines, in the midst of which is a line of lattice-filled diamonds or lozenges; each alternate rectangle occupied with a pointed quatrefoil, the points shaded with oblique strokes, and between each two points a rosette of dots; the alternate rectangles, with chequer-work. Flaring lip with horizontal bands about it, and a zone of vertical strokes at the top. Figured, or animal, decoration on the cover: on the principal zone about the amphora part, and between its two horizontal handles, on each side two long-legged horses feeding, one with his head close to his hind feet; under the body of each horse the figure often called a swastika, with arms so inclined, and the ends of each arm coming so near the next angle, that they look almost like diamonds with diagonals. Above, interrupting the bands about the body, and opposite the base of the vertical handle, the figure of a long-necked and long-tailed bird, above and below which is a rosette of dots. Figured, or animal decoration on the body: The handles furnish the best starting point. These all differ more or less from one another. Beginning with that shown nearly at the centre of Plate CIV., there are two divisions, above and below, each occupied by a feeding horse, beneath which is a long-legged, long-necked bird, of the stork or crane kind; one standing erect, the other dressing its plumage; a rosette of dots above and one below the bird; a rosette also in each right hand corner of the lower division. The rest of the ornamentation, in transverse lines, rows of dots and of vertical strokes, is seen well enough in the plate. Passing around to the left, the next handle, whose edge only is seen in the plate, the occupations of the birds are reversed; the upper one dressing its plumage, the lower one standing erect; two six-rayed stars replace the rosettes in the lower space, there being no rosettes in the upper. Also, sharp close zigzags take the place of the transverse lines of dots at the middle (as seen on the handle shown at centre of Plate CV.),

partment, seen on the left in Plate CIV. (which is the most elaborate of all), the deer not suckling is an antlered male (and perhaps this is the case in all the others ; but not certainly so except in that one shown on the right in Plate CIV.) ; the recumbent fawn on the left has above him a number of lines with pinnate strokes (like that hanging in each of the side compartments, but finer), looking much like twigs of weeping willow, and before him another, partially coiled. This decoration occurs in none of the other compartments. There are ten dot-rosettes ; in the next (left on Pl. CIV.), five rosettes and an eleven-rayed star ; the diamond filled in by lines parallel to all their sides. The next central compartment to the left (the right on Plate CV.) has six rosettes.; the next (the left on Plate CV.) has seven rosettes, a compound diamond divided into four parts by central lines parallel to the sides, and the parts filled in like lattice by smaller lines in like directions ; the next (the right on Plate CIV.) has five rosettes and one eleven-rayed star,. a diamond with diagonals, and in each triangle thus formed a stroke parallel to the adjacent side. The reclining fawns in the corners are in various attitudes. In the side compartments, many-rayed stars replace the dot-rosettes over the mallet or bipennis in some instances ; but in that one shown at the extreme left on Plate CIV., they are replaced by a leafy circular or hoop-wreath, which extends from the upper end of the handle of the bipennis to its head. Some of the horses have a visible mane ; others lack it. The lower animal zone has a division mark, seen nearly in the centre of Plate CIV., consisting of a single pinnate hanging. The zone comprises twenty-five feeding horses, with a dot-rosette between each two, at the top. On the left of the division mark, the first six horses have beneath them the figure often called the swastika, in nearly diamond shape, and a varying number of dot-rosettes (four with the first, three with the second, two each with the third, fourth, and fifth, and one with the sixth). The remaining nineteen horses have beneath them each a bird, of the sort already mentioned ; the attitudes of the birds varying greatly ; some standing erect, some arranging their plumage, some feeding, and one standing with his neck bent back and his head up. With each bird (except where pretty certainly obliterated) there are at least two rosettes, one above and one below. Found broken in many pieces, and reset.

and another zigzag band crosses at the bottom. The next handle is that shown at centre of Plate CV., where both birds are picking food from the ground ; two rosettes appear in the upper division, and three in the lower ; a band of large dots occurs just above the top band of lines visible on the plate ; zigzags in the middle band, but neither dots nor zigzags in the lowest. The fourth, or last, handle differs from all the others ; having, in place of the horses and birds, eight-pointed foliate patterns, like those in the zone above the handles, with a small circle between each two points. Between these the space is wider than on the figure-divisions of the other handles, and is occupied by two diagonals ; the angles vertically opposite being occupied with small circles, those horizontally opposite by nests of angles formed by lines parallel to the two diagonals. Close at each side of each handle is an ornament of two sets of vertical lines, extending from top to bottom of the zone, and between each two sets a vertical line of latticed diamonds, the angles between them on each side occupied by a very small circle. The four parts into which the handles divide the zone are occupied each by the same general design, yet with minor variations. Above, separated from the lower part by horizontal triple lines, a wide crenelated figure, shaded by parallel oblique strokes. The lower part is divided into three divisions or compartments, separated by bars of sets of vertical lines with a close zigzag between ; the side compartments having like decoration or ceiling above. In the central compartment is a branching, leafy tree, on which, at each side, two deer stand feeding, each with one foreleg raised against the tree ; the doe on the left suckles a fawn ; in each of the top corners is a reclining fawn (evidently intended to be in the background, but actual perspective is wanting) ; a number of rosettes of dots, and a diamond with diagonals, also are seen. The side compartments show each a standing horse, fastened by a halter to a manger-like projection on the side of the compartment next the central one, from which projection a line with pinnate downward oblique strokes hangs to the bottom of the compartment. Beneath the horse is a bird, of the kind previously described, with a rosette of dots above and one below it. From the ceiling hangs a thick line, with a horizontal figure at its lower end, the whole looking like an immense *bipennis*, or perhaps a beetle or mallet, with head enlarged at the ends, and an ornament, usually a rosette of dots, above each end of the mallet-head. The chief differences are as follows : In the central com-

# PLATE CVI.

857, 858.  Opposite sides of the same object.  Red ware ; exterior now brownish gray. Extreme height, 9½ inches.  Found at Citium.

Vase like a pitcher (large œnochoë, or even hydria); body of graceful ovoid shape, compressed at the ends ; mouth compressed at the sides so as to form a nozzle in front; handle joining lip, but rising at the bend a little higher than the lip.  Vase colored with some light ground color; decorations mostly in brown with some admixture of red.  Rather heavy band at junction of short neck with body ; above this a band of close zigzag; still above this a fine band about the neck, interrupted by a small nest of concentric circles at the points where the side is compressed; and last, a fine band close about the lip.  Handle decorated on the back, down and over its length, with two shallow gutters, which are colored brown, and united by a shading of transverse lines through their whole length. About the base of the handle is a heart-shaped mass of color, whose point is lengthened to reach within an inch of the bottom of the vase.  Directly opposite the handle, and beneath the spout, is one of those representations (scarcely seen at all in the plate) of a conventional lotus flower which remind somewhat of the Assyrian sacred tree, but pretty thoroughly disguised with modification from Egyptian *motifs*.  The central outline is a couple of lines like the sides of a trumpet, rising from near the base, flaring out at the top on the shoulder of the vase ; their ends joining two lines (that are convex upwards) that meet between the two first, a little above where the latter begin to flare ; the outline being that of the trumpet-shaped calyx of a flower, but yet having slightly the appearance of a palm tree.  In the space at the top, between the branches of the figure, is a vertical diamond, its sides double, the inner space divided into four smaller diamonds by lines passing through the centre parallel to the sides ; these smaller lozenges colored alternately red and brown.  Above and about this diamond are the petals of the immense flower, colored within

*PLATE CVI. CONTINUED.*

brown and red alternately.  The stem or trunk, included between the two lines first mentioned, is shaded below by transverse lines, each like a figure 3 lying on its convex side ;  then by straight transverse lines, as far as where the two inner lines of the outline meet each other ; these transverse lines being interrupted at a point about midway of the vertical space occupied by them, by three short vertical lines, making four little squares, of which the alternate ones are colored red.  From the base of the stem, on either side, project two smaller stems, each bearing a pair of ovate lanceolate leaves on pedicels (opposite on one stem, alternate on the other), and a petaled flower of a bell-shaped outline, its sepals colored red, its petals brown.  Above these project two blunt branches from the main stem, one on each side, nearly horizontally, but with a slightly upward curve ;  formed of a fine-lined outline shaded with transverse (vertical) strokes, their rounded ends solid brown.  Just above these, an ellipse with very wide border, within which are three others concentric of fine lines ;  the centre being covered by the stem ;  and at the top of the ellipse, two solid blunt projections on either side, a little longer than those below ; just above these, a pair of blunt branches like the first pair mentioned, but of the length of the solid ones last mentioned ;  then another ellipse of broad border, with three others, concentric, within ;  the latter not accurately drawn ;  the top of the outer ellipse coinciding almost exactly with the highest straight line of the shading of the main stem.  Above this is another pair of blunt branches, but curving downwards about the ellipse, their ends almost meeting those of the pair last above mentioned, which they exactly resemble in structure.  Out of each of them, above, springs another petaled flower of bell-shaped outline, and a pair of ovate lanceolate leaves ;  differing from the other pair only in having a band of three fine brown lines about the flower, just below its greater expansion.  Near the lower end of each springs out a bell-shaped, elongated, opening bud ; that on the right hand side larger than that on the left.  Both these upper flowers are shown in No. 857 ; and one of them in No. 858.  The four flowers remind one somewhat of the conventional rose of the Rhodian stamps ; and also of some species of clematis.

On the left hand side (No. 857), near the above design, is a bird whose shape is seen in the plate ; the lower claw almost touching the lower ellipse above mentioned ; its bill is almost

*PLATE CVI. CONTINUED.*

like that of a pelican (without the pouch beneath). It would seem that this bird is intended to be represented with two pairs of wings. The smaller wing on the nearer side is closed; of the larger pair, one wing is stretched on high, the other below; roughly fashioned like the wings of some Assyrian deities; but the feathers differently wrought. The lighter portions of both wings, perhaps of the tail also, were colored red. The bird has a crest, at first recurved, and then curved forward in a spiral. Its head comes under the upper flower of the branch above mentioned; its beak over the smaller and lower flower. Behind the bird is an antlered stag, grazing; its head, all but one antler, concealed behind the large down-stretched wing of the bird. On its shoulder and flank are Assyrian-like rosettes, the alternate petals of each colored red, and a dark brown ring plainly visible about the outermost light ring, although against a brown background. On the side, between two sets of red and brown lines, some light markings that may have imitated cuneiform script. Tail, a brown outline. The wing that is visible proceeds from the side next the spectator, as can plainly be seen on the object by the darker brown strokes, and the remnants of red, on the brown ground. The part shaded with finer lines seems to have been once colored red. From the shoulders springs a branch with two pairs of leaves; one pair lanceolate, the other obovate; and a great flower above, little different from the others; its outline more abruptly flaring and bell-shaped. On the right hand side (No. 858), a bird similar to that already described, and in like position and attitude; the red color still plainly discernible in the lighter portions of wings and tail. Behind it a stag, in motion like the other, but with very thick neck, raised high, and bent around so that the head looks backward. It has no antlers, but a beard like a goat's. The wing (probably on the side away from the spectator) is shorter, smaller, and not raised so high. The imitation of an inscription on the side is in a light rectangle. From the band about the base of the neck of the vase depend, on either side, near the extremities of the great flower beneath the spout, small rectangles in brown with transverse decorations like those first mentioned on the main stem near its base.

Broken in many places, and reset. Some small pieces still missing.

859, 860. Opposite sides of the same object. Red ware, exterior now gray. Height, 9¼ inches. Found at Golgoi (?) or Citium.

*PLATE CVI. CONTINUED.*

Vase like a pitcher (œnochoë), in shape like No. 857, 858 ; its minor decorations also similar, except that a rather wide red band replaces the finer brown one above the zigzag about the neck ; and below the back of the handle, near the point of the lengthened heart-shaped decoration, a wing spreads from either side (the end of one of them is seen in No. 859), in structure like the upper wing of the bird, except that the transverse lines give way to a zigzag at one point, and to a series of six small rectangles at another ; the alternate rectangles colored red. Also, above them, the heart-shaped decoration is ornamented by a horizontal light colored line, with a row of light colored dots beneath it ; and still below, two lines of light color converging to a point beneath, and enclosing a triangular space of red.

Below the nozzle is a conventional lotus, whose main outline is like the corresponding one in Nos. 857, 858, but the stem shorter, and the outer branching ends larger ; these last colored red within ; but the stem shaded with transverse lines, except at two places where they give place to rectangles, of which the alternate ones are colored red. At the top, the space between the branching ends is occupied partly by transverse lines, above the last two of which is a row of transverse strokes, and still above is an isosceles triangle, with two parallel angles within it, the innermost triangle filled with lozenge chequer-work. About the triangle are sharp petals, red and brown alternately. From the top of the triangle, a slender upright stem, two buds branching from the sides, and a bell-shaped petaled flower at the top. Below, the stem has one pair of blunt branches, then a broad margined ellipse with five others concentric within, of fine lines ; then a pair of recurved blunt branches, from either of which springs a stem and small bell-shaped flower—all nearly as in Nos. 857, 858.

On either side of this central object, a female figure, the body seen in front view, the feet pointed towards the object, the head averted ; one hand (the left in No. 859, the right in 860) closed, and raised just above the bud on its side of the central high flower-stalk ; the other hand holding the end of one of the main branches of the principal stem. Dress of each figure, a long-sleeved robe, reaching nearly to the feet ; ornamented border at the bottom, ornamental girdle with long tasselled end ; ornamental collar ; necklace with large pendant brooch, or elliptical medallion, hung by the ends ; armlets ; bracelets ; all colored brown, with

*PLATE CVI. CONTINUED.*

light stripes, except the robe, which is red. Head, eyes, coiffure, and general style of figure, Egyptian.

On the left-hand side (Plate 859), a bird, with two pairs of wings, in attitude as shown in No. 859; a flower-like crest on its head ; from its neck extends upwards (apparently grasped in its beak) a flower like a calystegia, the outer calyx immensely exaggerated ; below the beak hangs another flower-stem, with a pair of leaves (colored red) and another unopened flower with great calyx, or else a second pair of leaves. In the bird's talons (which are only two to each foot), with one foot it holds a stem with one bell-shaped petaled flower, and one bud. The smaller wing, the tail, and perhaps also the larger wings, of bird, with lighter spaces, colored red ; flowers held by the talons, partially colored red.

On the right-hand side (Plate 860), a bird of similar sort ; but in a different attitude ; its crest recurved below, and then curved forward in a spiral ; below which last is a projection some-what like the upper process of a toucan's beak, but really behind the head. The talon holds a flower-stalk with pair of blunt leaves, a pair of large calices (or perhaps differently shaped leaves), and a petaled, bell-shaped flower. Light spaces on wing and tail of bird, colored red ; as are also some of the flower petals.

Vase broken in many pieces, and reset. A few pieces still missing.

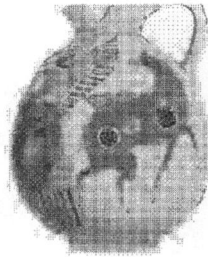

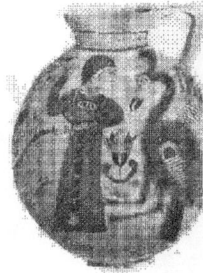

THE GF?

# PLATE CVII.

Large vases, generally amphora-shaped, but with a low foot; handles set with their ends in the same horizontal line; large necks, enlarging towards the top and flaring at the mouth. Ground color gray; decorations in brown. Inside the lip, a double band; and on the flat edge, a zigzag band. The band about the foot is nearly obliterated in all. Outside of the handles colored; about the base of each a mass of color ending in a point below. Necks a mass of solid color, except a light band under the lip or rim (out of sight in the plate), and a zone a little above the middle, consisting of two bands of finer or coarser horizontal circles, between which is a band of diamonds. About the body, various bands, as shown in the respective figures; the main differences occurring in the zone which contains the handles, and in that on the shoulder above them. All found at Dali Potamia.

861. Gray ware. Height, 24 inches.

Zone on the shoulder with four nearly equidistant triangles, whose base is the band at bottom of zone, and its apex at the band above, shaded within by lines parallel to the two sides; also lines parallel to each side without. Handle zone, on each side, midway between the handles, two rudely square spaces, separated and bounded by sets of vertical lines; within each another rude square inscribed, which is divided into chequer-work; the dark chequers shaded by lines parallel to the two sides. Outside of the whole figure, two vertical wavy lines; but these wavy lines are wanting on the side of the vase not shown in the plate.

862. Gray ware. Height, 24 inches.

No decoration on shoulder zone. Handle zone: a simple, irregular, wavy line.

863. Red ware, exterior now salmon-gray. Height, 24¾ inches.

Shoulder zone, six triangular shaded spaces, nearly equal distances apart, similar to those described at No. 861, but without the external lines there mentioned. Handle zone, on each side, midway between the handles, a single square space like those which are double in No. 861;

*PLATE CVII. CONTINUED.*

and bounded by straight and wavy lines, as shown in the plate. In the top corners of the square is the figure often called a *swastika*, those on one side showing a difference in direction of revolution, but those on the other side an agreement.

864. Gray ware. Height, 28 inches.

Shoulder zone with triangular figures like those of No. 861, alternating with a figure composed of a set of vertical straight lines with a nearly semicircular piece of solid color on each side. Handle zone, in squares, diagonals, and shaded diamonds, as shown in the plate. Broken, and reset.

# Plate CVIII.

Great amphora-shaped vases, with a low foot; handles set and decorated as in Plate CVII., but each handle has a rounded projection on the top; neck nearly cylindrical; large rounded rim at the top. Ground color gray; decoration in brown. All have a band inside the lip, a zigzag about the rim; a band about the foot, though that is almost entirely obliterated in all; and in the handle zone, a rather fine but very irregular wavy line extending from handle to handle on each side; bands about the neck and body; all of which are sufficiently shown in the plates. The chief difference consists in the middle zone of the neck. All found at Dali Potamia.

865. Gray ware. Height, 28¼ inches.

Neck zone, alternate vertical pairs of concentric circle patterns and rudely square spaces, bounded by sets of lines, and having rude double diagonals. At one point this square is replaced by a simple set of vertical lines; so that there are six pairs of the circle patterns and but five of the squares. Small hole in one side, made by decay, or possibly breakage.

866. Gray ware. Height, 26¼ inches.

Zone about the neck, four squares bounded by sets of vertical lines, and filled in with triangular spaces, black or shaded by lines parallel to the sides, broad light diagonal bands, and a central lozenged diamond. Between each two of these squares are vertical pairs of concentric-circle patterns, the pairs separated by vertical pinnate twigs. The number in each space varies (as the squares are not equidistant), being four each in two of the spaces, three in another, and two in another.

867. Gray ware. Height, 28 inches.

Neck zone, six squares somewhat similar to those on No. 866, with concentric circles and vertical pinnate twigs between, as in No. 866. But in the two spaces shown on the plate the arrangement is irregular. In the other four there are simply two vertical pairs of the circle patterns, with one pinnate twig between them.

868. Gray ware. Height, 28¼ inches.

Neck with a single band of concentric-circle patterns.

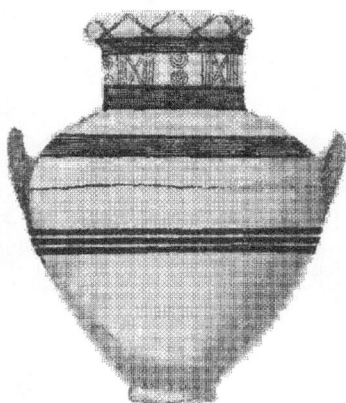

# PLATE CIX.

869. Reddish ware, exterior now gray. Height, 27 inches. Found at Dali Potamia.

Vase of the kind described in Plate CVIII. Neck zone, vertically arranged pairs of concentric-circle patterns, alternating with a vertical feathery twig.

870. Yellowish-brown ware; surface colored grayish white. Height, 6¼ inches. Found at Alambra.

Vase (œnochoë) not made on a wheel; decoration of brown lines and geometrical patterns, as shown in the plate. This differs so slightly from the object at Plate LXXXVI., No. 760, and again from that at Plate CXIII., No. 886, that the same description will serve for all three.

871. Brown ware. Height, 28 inches. Found at Ormidia.

Large vase (amphora) with low foot; handles joined in a horizontal line; neck enlarging upward; flat rim about mouth. Inside, two brown bands below the mouth; several sets of broad marks on the rim in the direction of radii. Handles colored brown, their ends in a long-pointed patch of color. Bands of brown about body and neck; other decoration: on the neck, guilloche enclosing red spaces, and a band of tongue-pattern below; between them a zone of conventional lotus flowers alternating with buds; all colored red. On the shoulder, a zone of somewhat conventional red lotus flowers alternate with brown buds; the buds, and also the flowers, being connected together by festooned stems; the two sets of loops intersecting.

872. Gray ware. Height, 28 inches. Found at Ormidia.

Large vase of same general description as those represented on Plate CVII. Shoulder zone like No. 863, Plate CVII., except that midway between, but higher up than, the handles, on each side, in the midst of an ellipse of solid color, a rounded, lengthened prominence replaces two of the triangular colored spaces. Handle zone, with geometrical patterns as shown in the plate; but on the opposite side, not shown in the plate, the two squares are separated by a third,

*PLATE CIX. CONTINUED.*

which latter has merely double diagonals, like one of those on Plate CVII., No. 864 ; while outside of the whole figure, at each end, is an ornamental lozenge border like the central pattern of
No. 864 ; outside of which, again, are wavy lines. About the body of the vase are a few traces
of incised lines, doubtless made when on the wheel. Decoration within as in No. 871.

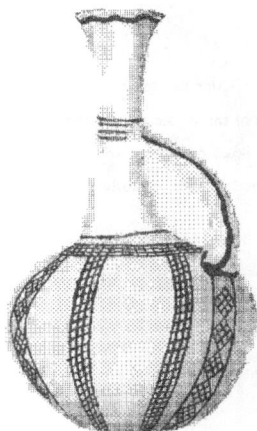

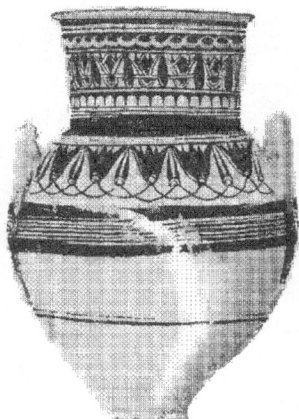

# PLATE CX.

873. Red ware, exterior now gray. Height, 27½ inches. Found at Ormidia.

Large amphora-shaped vase, with low foot; side handles joined horizontally; neck nearly cylindrical, contracting upwards, but expanding at the mouth. Ground color gray; decoration in geometrical patterns in brown and red, as shown in the plate. Decoration on rim and inside, as in No. 872. Much cracked, and a few small chips broken away.

874. Red ware. Height, 29¼ inches. Found at Ormidia.

Amphora-shaped vase, of same general form as the last, but body more rapidly tapering downward, and neck rapidly expanding upwards. Inside and rim decoration as in No. 873. Ground color gray. Neck zone decorated with geometrical patterns in brown and red; handle zone also with concentric-circle patterns, as shown in the plate. Cracked; piece broken out at top.

875. Red ware, exterior now gray. Height, 14 inches. Found at Alambra.

Handled vase with ovate body, cylindrical neck, slightly flaring mouth. Ground color light gray; decorations very light reddish brown, in bands about neck and shoulder; vertical bands of lines alternate with single wavy lines. Very slightly chipped at the mouth.

876. Red ware, exterior colored gray. Height, 16½ inches. Found at Dali Potamia.

Amphora-shaped vase, but inclining to the form of a crater; flaring foot; handles set on vertically, joining the rim; neck with slightly curved outline, but nearly cylindrical. Inside the lip, band of brown; on rim, zigzag with ornamental bands; outside, zigzag down handle, with curve below it on body, like the hanging horns of a gnu; other decorations in geometrical patterns, as shown in the plate.

877. Red ware, exterior colored gray. Height, 22 inches. Found at Dali Potamia.

Amphora-shaped vase, whose shape and general decoration are well shown in the plate. The neck zone is occupied by three patterns, of which one only is seen completely in the plate. Handles, rim, and inside decorated like the other great amphora vases.

# PLATE CXI.

---

Large vases of the same general shape as those figured on Plate CIX., No. 871, and Plate CX., Nos. 873, 877 ; inside and rim similarly decorated. All but No. 881 of red ware, with a ground coloring of gray ; decoration in brown and red, as shown in the plates ; also a brown band, not much obliterated, about the foot. All found at Ormidia.

878. Height, 27¼ inches.

The pattern seen in front view on the neck zone is repeated on the opposite side. The intervening spaces have a pattern like that seen on the middle of the shoulder zone, but more expanded.

879. Height, 28¼ inches.

Besides the decoration visible on the neck zone, there is a pattern directly above each handle like that seen on the shoulder zone toward either side. On the side opposite that seen in the plate, two of the so-called swastikas, instead of three.

880. Height, 27¼ inches.

So nearly like No. 873 on Plate CX., that the same description will serve for both. Broken, and reset. Small chips broken off the rim.

881. Gray ware. Height, 28¼ inches.

Besides the decoration visible on the plate, that on the neck zone, on the opposite side, has pendant feathery twigs, like those seen on No. 880.

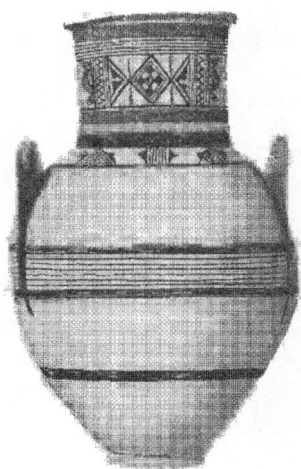

# PLATE CXII.

Vases of same general description as those of Plate CXI.; but with additional decorations, chiefly of lotus flowers much modified and conventionalized; sometimes suggesting an asclepias in seed; and sometimes the Assyrian sacred tree, toward which last there are various steps of approach in the decorations of different vases. All have the same decoration within, and (except No. 884) on the rim, as No. 873, Plate CX.; none have a band of color on the foot. All are of red ware, with a ground coloring of gray. All found at Ormidia.

882. Height, 26 inches.

Decoration of circular bands; on the neck, zones of rosettes alternating with geometrical patterns, and a zone of lozenge and chequer-work; on the main zone of the body, conventionalized lotus flowers and buds, the stems of the buds uniting in one series of festoons; those of the flowers in another. On the neck zone, directly over each handle, but invisible in the plate, a large conventional flower with a chequer-work triangle among the petals.

883. Height, 27 inches.

Neck zone with highly conventionalized lotus flower, as shown on the plate. Over each handle, a figure like those on the sides of the shoulder zone of Plate CXI., No. 879, but more elaborate.

884. Height, 29 inches.

Decoration of neck and shoulder zones in concentric-circle patterns and conventional lotuses; the largest of the latter on the shoulder zone having rosettes and lozenge-chequers among the petals, and concentric-circle patterns under the artificially curled outer leaves; the larger ones on the neck zone having only the rosettes; the smaller ones on both zones, only the lozenge-chequers. Cracked, but not broken.

885. Height, 32¼ inches.

Decoration with circular bands and lines; lozenge and chequer patterns; and conventional lotus flowers and buds; as shown in the plate. Buds, flowers, and stems on the shoulder zone less conventionalized than in No. 882.

# PLATE CXIII.

886. Red ware, colored white and decorated with brown. Height, 6¼ inches. Found at Alambra.

Vase (œnochoë) of almost exactly the same description as the objects Plate LXXXVI., No. 760, and Plate CIX., No. 870, which see.

887, 889, 890. Large vases of same general style and description as those of Plate CXII., but decorated on the outside with circular bands and lines in red and brown, and concentric-circle patterns in brown. None have a band of color about the foot. All of red ware, with a ground coloring of gray. All found at Limbia, between Alambra and Dali.

887. Height, 25¾ inches.

889. Height, 25½ inches.

890. Height, 27½ inches.

888. Red ware. Length, 15½ inches. Found at Dali.

Probably a sconce, or hanging lamp-support or socket. Shape long and flat, ends rounded, sides not straight; hole for suspension, below which is a bull's head, decorated with red and brown. Decoration of flat surface, in colored diamonds, chequers, lozenges, and points. At bottom, a roughly semi-cylindrical shelf, projecting 3½ inches, whose decoration without is in diaper work of squares with diagonals; within, of strokes. On the flat surface, within the circle of the shelf, a rude figure in red and brown, which seems to be a fish.

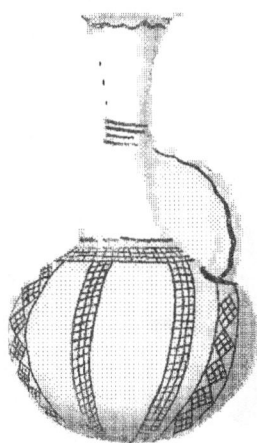

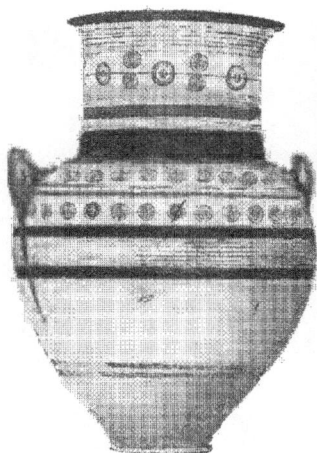

# PLATE CXIV.

---

All of red ware, with a ground color at present gray; decoration in red and brown. All found at Ormidia, except No. 893, which was found at Dali.

891. Height, 7½ inches.

Vase with foot and handles (cylix); decoration with circular bands and geometrical patterns, birds, and conventional lotus flowers, as shown in the plate. Broken, and reset.

892. Height, 6¼ inches.

Vase (cylix) of shape much like the last; decoration in circular bands and other geometrical patterns; with highly conventionalized lotus flower between the handles—which has a triangle of chequer-work among the petals.

893. Height, 10 inches.

Nearly obovate vase with side handles and light foot (stamnos); decorated with fan-like lines on the handles; circular bands, and other geometrical patterns; and conventional lotus flowers between the handles. Slightly broken, and reset.

894. Height, 8⅝ inches.

Amphora vase; low foot; decoration with circular bands, wavy lines, chequer-work and other geometrical patterns; panels with lotus flowers near the handles.

895. Height, 9½ inches.

Vase of nearly the same shape as the last; on the shoulder zone an eight-pointed star; on each side of it a rectangle seeming to contain an imitation of a cuneiform inscription.

# PLATE CXV.

All of red ware, with a ground coloring of gray, and decoration in brown and red. All except 898, cylices of the same general shape as those figured on Plate CXIV. Inside decoration of all, more or less elaborate, in bands or lines. All found at Ormidia.

896. Height, 5½ inches.

Decoration in geometrical patterns, rosettes, and large conventional lotus flowers.

897. Height, 4¾ inches.

Decoration, geometrical patterns; a rude flying bird; and so-called swastikas. Broken, and reset.

898. Height, 8¾ inches.

Amphora vase, of shape much like those on Plate CXIV. Decoration in geometrical patterns, and a seven-pointed star, as shown in the plate.

899. Height, 4¼ inches.

Decoration in conventional and geometrical patterns, as shown in the plate.

900. Height, 4¼ inches.

Decoration in geometrical patterns and circular bands; the six-pointed star made by circular arcs drawn free-hand.

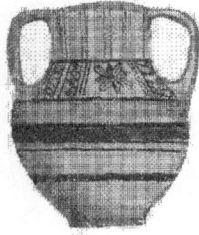

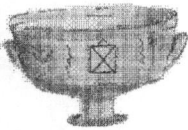

# PLATE CXVI.

Large vases of red ware ; body nearly obovate, or reversed pear-shape ; ground color of all apparently red. All are probably within the class or kind called amphora ; though they may be (especially No. 903) of the class called stamnos. All found at Curium.

901. Height, 12¾ inches.

Thick foot, flaring at base ; narrow cylindrical ring at mouth ; handles set vertically, furrowed. Decoration, mere bands or lines about the vase, with also, on the handle zone, three large brown discs in a horizontal line, on each side.

902. Height, 15 inches.

Very low foot ; neck short, with flat rim. Handles set horizontally, furrowed ; and from the top of each an auxiliary handle extends to the rim. Piece broken away on the rim.

903. Height, 14 inches.

Foot large, bell-shaped ; handles set horizontally ; mouth a large beaded rim. Decorated with horizontal bands and zones of concentric-circle patterns. Chipped slightly on the foot.

904. Height, 19 inches.

Rather high, flaring foot ; very short, cylindrical neck, and wide rim. Handles set vertically, and joining the lip ; furrowed. Slightly chipped on the rim ; foot broken, and reset.

PLATE CXVII.

All of red ware ; colored and decorated.

905.   Height, 18 inches.   Found at Ormidia.

Amphora ; ground color gray ; decoration in horizontal bands and zones of concentric-circle patterns.   Rim and inside decorated like those of Plate CXI.

906.   Height, 25 inches.   Found at Dali.

Amphora, or perhaps stamnos.   Ground color gray on handles and neck, red on body ; decoration in horizontal bands, and zones of concentric-circle and geometrical patterns.

907.   Height, 10¾ inches.   Found at Curium (Episcopi).

Vase of irregular obovate body, flaring foot (into which liquid can be poured and retained, as in Plate XCV., Nos. 813, 815) ; spout a long tapering pipe or nose, at whose base eyes and spreading horns are wrought in relief (on the body of the vase) ; the nose having also a bridle indicated on it in brown.   At top the vase has a false neck (closed), fashioned into a female head, which is joined by the handle from behind.   About this head is a fillet, below which the hair is seen in short curls.   Hair is wrought above, and in long heavy curls at the sides. Necklace (in relief and colored) about the neck ; breasts indicated by prominences on the body of the vase.   Decoration in geometrical and other patterns, as shown in the plate.   Small pieces chipped away at the foot.

908.   Height, 10⅝ inches.   Found at Dali.

Ovoid vase with flat bottom ; neck fashioned into a female head, with cincture and long curls like lappets ; large eyes, nose, and ears ; bead necklace, colored brown ; mouth of vase on top of head ; two short tapering spouts take the place of rude breasts.   Decoration in circular bands of red and brown, concentric circles and geometrical patterns, as shown in the plate.

# PLATE CXVIII.

All of red ware, having a ground coloring of gray ; decoration in brown and red.

909. Height, 8 inches. Found at Ormidia.

Vase with ovoid body, flat bottom, cylindrical neck, and flaring lip, which is joined by the handle. A little to the left of the handle, or less than ¼ the circumference from it, a short, stout, tapering spout. Decoration in circular bands, rosettes, and geometrical patterns ; as shown in the plate. Part of lip broken away.

910. Height, 7 inches. Found at Ormidia.

Amphora, with short flaring foot. Neck and shoulder zones with a decoration that seems made with a brush (or comb) used generally for concentric circles, and resembles locks of curly hair. Guilloche between neck and shoulder zones. Large dent in lower part of body, made while the clay was soft.

911. Height, 9⅝ inches. Found at Curium.

Œnochoë, with a nearly globular body. Mouth compressed at the sides, so as to form a nozzle opposite the handle. Decoration, concentric-circle patterns, bands, and a bearded, helmeted head.

912. Height, 8 inches. Found at Ormidia.

Amphora, with flaring foot; decoration in circles and geometrical patterns, as shown in the plate.

913. Height, 8 inches. Found at Ormidia.

Amphora, with oval body and flaring foot. Decoration, circular bands ; guilloche, and neck zone of fretted, pointed oval or flabellum patterns, as shown in the plate.

# PLATE CXIX.

---

Pitcher-shaped vases (œnochoæ), with nearly globular bodies, flat bottoms with very small bead; lip compressed at the sides to form a nozzle opposite the handle; all decorated with concentric-circle patterns; bands about neck and lip; and stripes on the handles. All of red ware.

914. Height, 8 inches. Found at Dali.

Below the neck, opposite the handle, a long triple cross like the cypriote character *a*; on the shoulder zone, a cross of wedges, like the spokes of a wheel, in the centre of the concentric-circle pattern.

915. Height, 8 inches. Found at Dali.

Has decoration below the spout like that of No. 914.

916. Height, 12½ inches. Found between Larnaka proper and Kiti.

Has its principal bands and circles in white.

917. Height, 12¼ inches. Found at Dali.

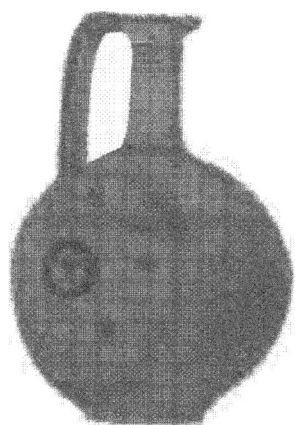

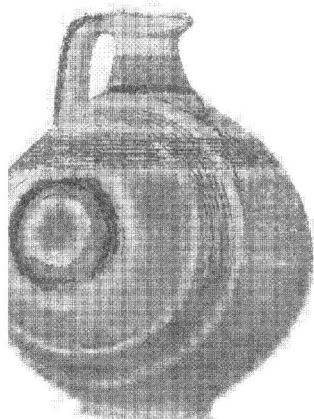

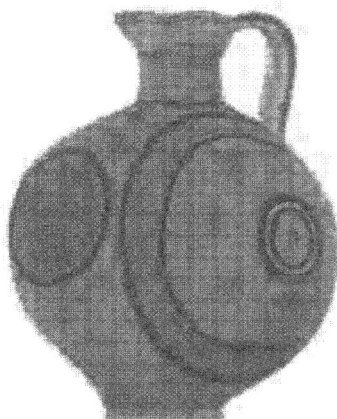

# PLATE CXX.

---

All of fine red ware ; of nearly globular body ; with handle and neck ; all decorated with concentric-circle patterns and circular bands.  All found at Dali.

918.  Height, 6 inches.

Aryballos, of nearly ellipsoidal shape (the end turned toward the spectator), its ends almost flat-conical.  Neck funnel-shaped, with a ridge at about ⅓ its height.  Besides the concentric-circle patterns, there are other decorations not visible on the plate ; two bands of very fine lines about the body at either side of the neck ; between which, reaching from neck to middle of body, two parallel angles, joined by a vertical line of alternate lozenges, ending in a half lozenge.  Wedge-shaped piece broken out at top of neck, above the handle.

919.  Height, 8¼ inches.

Pitcher-shaped vase with globular body (aryballos ?) ; with long neck surmounted by a cow's head.

920.  Height, 8 inches.

Œnochoë.  Body slightly ovate, with flat bottom ; compressed at side to join a nozzle. It has also the peculiar decoration of No. 914, Plate CXIX.

921.  Height, 6¼ inches.

Vase with body nearly globular ; cylindrical neck, with a shoulder near the top.  On the sides, light colored wheel-hub and spokes left in dark circle.  (Above this, three concentric-circle patterns not shown in the plate.)

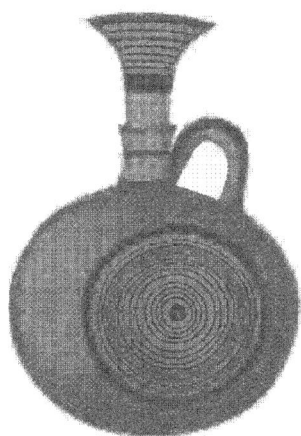

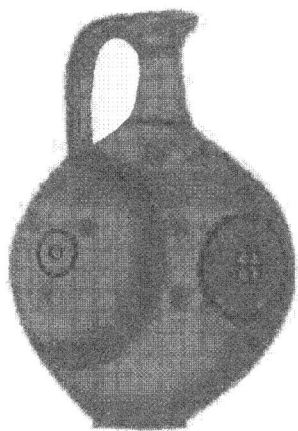

www.ingramcontent.com/pod-product-compliance
Lightning Source LLC
Chambersburg PA
CBHW030631270326
41927CB00007B/1395